CAT
QUILTS
AND CRAFTS

LaVERA LANGEMAN

Chilton Book Company
Radnor, Pennsylvania

Designed by Anthony Jacobson
Manufactured in the United States of America

Library of Congress Cataloging in Publication Data

Langeman, LaVera.
    Cat quilts & crafts / LaVera Langeman.
        p.   cm.
    ISBN 0-8019-8355-X
    1. Patchwork—Patterns.   2. Appliqué—Patterns.   3. Embroidery—
Patterns.   4. Cats in art.   I. Title: Cat quilts and crafts.
TT835.L333   1992
    746.46—dc20   92-8556
                                                                        CIP

1 2 3 4 5 6 7 8 9 0   1 0 9 8 7 6 5 4 3 2

CAT QUILTS AND CRAFTS

To my Mother whose life has

brought all of us

a lot of joy

CONTENTS

CAT QUILTS AND CRAFTS

INTRODUCTION

My wonderful seventh grade home economics teacher, Mrs. Righter, introduced me to sewing. My father, an art teacher, instilled in me a strong fundamental background in drawing and design. I spent many of my summer vacations with my aunt Eleanor on her small farm in British Columbia. I watched her plan and piece together quilts for the Island's annual fund-raising drive. They were always so beautiful!

As I got older, I learned by helping with a few stitches here and there. Both my ability and love for quilting grew. My first project was a small appliquéd pillow. I made it for my grandfather, who was ill at the time, and gave it to him in the quiet company of my Mennonite family. My relatives inspected every stitch, and as each person smiled approval, my pride and excitement grew. Soon my love of quilting became an abiding preoccupation.

While attending classes at the Fashion Institute of Technology in New York, I won scholarships and awards for my clothing designs. Soon I found myself absorbed in a fashion career. In my spare time I continued with my true love—quilting. I entered shows and won awards and soon quilting became more exciting than designing a line of clothing.

When I was expecting my son, my doctor advised me to give up my high-pressure fashion career. I began to think of ways to continue designing and quilting. My love of quilting and cats soon gave me the idea for this book.

Drew Weidenbacher, my husband, helped my ideas become reality with his love and support. We took pictures of cats everywhere we went until we had what we felt was a rich diversity of cats in different poses.

Special thanks to Sandy Davis. This book will give cat lovers a lot of ideas to create gifts and accessories to adorn their homes. A true cat lover can never have enough cat paraphernalia around. It will guide the beginner and when you want to set your imagination free, it will let you soar. I hope you will find in it as much enjoyment as I did creating it.

CHAPTER ONE

HOW TO USE THIS BOOK

The purpose of this book is to encourage you to create one-of-a-kind quilts, household items, clothing, and other crafts. There are thirty-seven different cat templates to choose from. Use them to create unique gifts such as pillows, tea cozies, dish towels, place mats, a sewing machine cover, and sweat shirts. Projects and templates for creating festive Christmas items such as a tree skirt and stocking, and other holiday items are also included. You can even customize the patterns to resemble your own beloved pet. Your imagination is the only limit.

For projects which are featured in the color section, I have provided a materials list and directions to make them as shown. I have also supplied suggestions on how to make them with alternate fabrics and color schemes. Remember, these are only suggestions; you should decide what colors and fabrics to use, and have fun doing it! Each chapter contains ideas for additional projects. The possibilities are endless.

When making patterns for large projects, you can use several sheets of newspaper taped together or several shopping bags cut apart, flattened, and taped together. Also, you are not restricted to using the templates as provided. Your local copy shop can reduce or enlarge them to fit your needs.

Getting Started

Choose an item that you would like to create and decide on a color scheme. When purchasing the fabrics, be sure that all yardage is from the same bolt. This ensures that all fabric is the same shade. Prewash fabrics to test for shrinkage and colorfastness. If you discover that your fabric is not colorfast, wash and dry it several times until the water runs clear.

After you have dried and pressed the fabric, cut out the blocks that you will use for the background of your appliqué. Decide whether you will be doing your appliqué by machine or by hand, then go to that section of the book. Remember when cutting out your blocks that the appliqué process causes the blocks to end up slightly smaller. Allow for this by adding an extra ½ inch to the seam allowance. When you have finished the appliqué, measure the block again and trim where needed.

Notions for Appliquéing

There are several products available in sewing supply stores to make appliquéing easier. *Fusibles* are used to hold appliqués to background fabrics and keep the edges firmly in place for the final stitching step. Stitch Witchery, Fine Fuse, Magic Polyweb, and Jiffy Fuse are commercial fusible webbings. They are placed between two pieces of fabric and pressed with a hot iron until the webbing melts and holds the two fabrics together.

Using an Appliqué Pressing Sheet or a Teflon sheet will protect your iron and allow you to press the fusible web to one fabric at a time. These sheets look like opaque wax paper, are reusable, and come in handy sizes.

The fastest method for fused appliqués is to use a paper-backed fusible webbing such as Pellon's Wonder-Under or Aleene's Hot Stitch. Press the rough side of the webbing to the wrong side of the fabric for three seconds with a hot, dry iron. Let the fabric cool. Draw your design on the paper backing and cut to the desired shape. After cutting, peel off the backing and position the appliqué, coated side down, on the background fabric. Place a damp cloth over it and press for ten seconds with iron on wool setting. Finish appliquéing by machine or hand.

Note: Shapes drawn on paper backing of fusible web will be reversed on the garment. Be sure to draw mirror images of letters or numbers.

Stabilizers are used behind fabric to keep it from puckering when you embroider. Tear-away stabilizers come in stiff or soft finishes and some can be ironed on. When embroidering, place them between the fabric and the machine. When the embroidery is completed, they tear away from the fabric easily.

Another type of stabilizer is a thin film of plastic which dissolves when wet. It is transparent and can be used on top of the embroidery as well. Clamp it into the hoop along with the fabric. When your embroidery is complete, rinse out the stabilizer with warm water. If you do not want to use a commercial stabilizer, try pinning the fabric to a piece of heavy paper (packing paper or a shopping bag will do). After embroidering, gently tear the paper away.

Note: Do not confuse stabilizers with interfacings. Interfacings are permanent and don't tear away. They are used to stabilize areas in a garment that are likely to stretch—armholes, necklines, cuffs, collars, etc.

An easy way to prevent appliqué pieces from fraying is to use spray starch and an iron on them before cutting out. This gives the fabric a crisp, sized finish that also makes the piece more substantial and easier to appliqué.

Hand Appliqué

To transfer the pattern that you have selected to the background fabric or square, place the fabric over the drawing and trace the image onto the fabric with a water soluble quilting pen or a very light pencil. If the fabric is too thick or too dark to see through, trace the image onto paper, cut it out, place this pattern on the right side of the fabric, and trace around it. This will give you a transfer guide to follow when you begin to appliqué (Fig. 1-1).

To make templates, place a piece of paper

Fig. 1-1. Create a transfer guide.

over the individual pieces of the pattern (Figs. 1-2 and 1-3). Numbering the templates and writing the numbers onto the transfer guide will help you with the placement when working with several templates. Lay each one on the right side of the fabric to be used for the appliqué and draw around it, adding a ¼ inch seam allowance. The seam allowance will be turned under when the piece is hemmed in place (Figs. 1-4 and 1-5). At

Fig. 1-2. Make individual templates.

Fig. 1-3. Cut and number the templates.

Fig. 1-4. Create the appliqué.

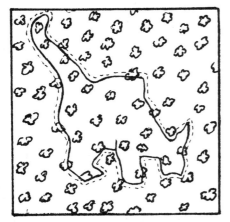

Fig. 1-5. Add a ¼ inch seam allowance to the appliqué.

this point make sure that the areas to be embroidered are clearly marked. Use a hoop to do any embroidery before cutting out the pieces.

When all the pieces have been cut out, place them on the background block and check the overlapping, deciding which piece needs to be sewn on first. Small appliqués, such as the inside of the cat's ear, should be sewn onto the head before the head is sewn onto the background block. Be sure to match the color of thread to the piece being sewn. Stitches should be ⅛ inch in length, except on curves and stress points where the stitching may be closer together.

Once you've determined which piece is going to be stitched on first, position it using the transfer guide you drew onto the block earlier. To hold the piece in place while turning the hems under, use a fusible, pin it, or baste an X in the middle of it. Use a blind stitch to turn your hems under (Fig. 1-6).

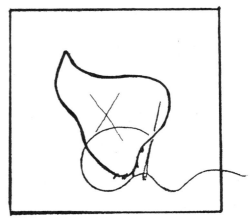

Fig. 1-6. Baste an X in the middle of the appliqué and use a blind stitch to turn the hems under.

Some appliqués have parts that extend beyond the edge of the background block. Stitch these pieces up to the seam allowance only. Fold the pieces that extend back onto themselves inside the square and pin (Fig. 1-7). These can then be sewn down onto the quilt once it has been put together.

Concave curves should be clipped in as few places as possible, but enough so that when the hem is turned under, it will lay flat (Fig. 1-8). Convex curves should not be clipped. This will only make stitching more difficult. Instead, pin these areas down in small sections and then work

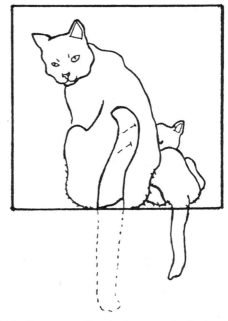

Fig. 1-7. Some appliqués have parts that extend beyond the background block.

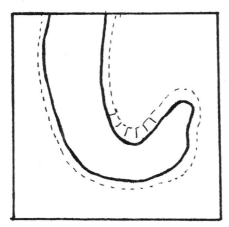

Fig. 1-8. Concave curves.

the hem under with your finger or a needle, until it lays smooth (Fig. 1-9). Points (Fig. 1-10) are achieved by folding the seam allowance under on one side and stitching that side from bottom to top. When you reach the top, clip the extra seam allowance (A). Fold down the point and tuck it under (B). Fold the seam allowance down on the other side and stitch it from top to bottom (C).

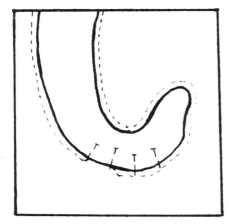

Fig. 1-9. Convex curves.

Fig. 1-10. How to sew points.

Machine Appliqué

The width of the zigzag stitch used depends on the weight of the fabric. The lighter the weight the narrower the stitch should be. Medium weight fabrics will require a wider stitch. Stitch length is also important. The stitches should be as close together as possible. Testing the stitches on a sample of the fabric is the only way to determine the perfect stitch.

Appliqués and templates are created the same way as for hand appliquéing, except seam allowances should not be added. Before cutting the appliqué to the finished size, fuse interfacing to the back of the fabric and embroider any details needed. When all the pieces are cut out, put them in place on the background block. Check overlapping. Baste pieces securely into place or glue down with a water soluble glue stick (the glue will wash out in the first washing). Make sure that the glue is thoroughly dry before stitching. You may also want to pin the square to a slightly larger piece of heavy paper to make sewing easier. Stitch down first the pieces that don't overlap the others, then gradually add and stitch down the overlapping pieces layer by layer.

Remember to cut and secure all the squares before starting to sew. Sew all the pieces that need the same color thread at the same time. This helps to cut down on the need to change thread so often. When turning the corners, leave the sewing machine needle in the background fabric. Raise the pressure foot and pivot the fabric. On the inside corners stitch 2 or 3 stitches past the corner and stop. Leave the needle in the fabric, raise the pressure foot, and pivot. When stitching around small curves and circles, do only six stitches at a time. Lift the pressure foot with the needle still in the fabric and pivot. Repeat these steps until the curve or circle is completely sewn.

Adding Lace and Ruffles

Adding lace trims and ruffles is done very much the same way. First determine the length you need by doubling the length or circumference of the piece. In the case of ruffles, you must also determine the width. This is a matter of personal taste (I usually use 2½ inches). Double the width

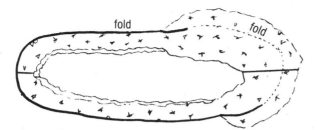

Fig. 1-11. Fold the ruffle lengthwise, right sides facing out.

you decide on and add ¹⁄₂ inch seam allowances (for example, a 2¹⁄₂ inch ruffle would require 6 inches of fabric).

Sew strips of fabric or lace, right sides together, at the ends to make a circle. With lace, a matching zigzag stitch will do nicely. Fold the ruffle lengthwise so that the right sides are out (see Fig. 1-11) and press.

Now sew the raw edge of your ruffle or lace on the seam allowance with a long single stitch. Use this stitch to gather by pulling the top thread while sliding the fabric inward. Sometimes when the piece is a long one, it helps to stitch in ten-inch increments and leave a thread hanging. Repeat for the entire length. Then gather these smaller areas. (Make sure to stop and start very close together!)

After gathering, place the ruffle against the raw edge of the piece you are working on in the area you want the ruffle to go. Adjust gathering to fit, then pin raw edges together. The ruffle will face "into" the project. Baste in place and sew.

If the project is a pillow, place the backing over the top piece and the ruffle, right sides together, and stitch on the seam allowance. (The ruffle will be in between the front and back right sides.) Remember to leave an opening to turn your pillow inside out. You can also add both the lace and the ruffle together by simply sewing the two together before gathering.

Mitering Corners

For mitered corners, start by placing a mark at the end of the seam lines ¹⁄₂ inch from the corners on the wrong side of the quilt. Stitch the top and bottom borders, stopping at these marks. Repeat for the sides. Press the borders right side up with the ends overlapping.

With right sides facing, pin adjacent borders at the corners on the wrong side then draw a 45°

angle, starting at the last stitch on the seams and going to the outside edge. (To get a 45° angle, fold a square piece of paper in half diagonally.) Stitch on this line, press open, and trim the excess fabric.

Helpful Embroidery Stitches

Fig. 1-12. *Outline Stitch.* Work from left to right, keeping the thread to the left of the needle. Use small stitches.

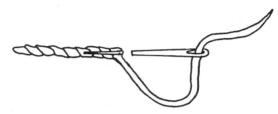

Fig. 1-13. *Backstitch.* Bring the needle up on the sewing line. Take small stitches, bringing the needle forward and up the same distance. Repeat.

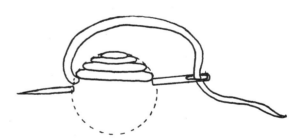

Fig. 1-14. *Horizontal Satin Stitch.* Use a straight stitch as close together as possible to fill the area needed. The surface should be smooth and the outside edges should be even.

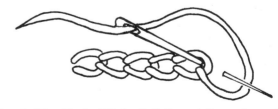

Fig. 1-15. *Chain Stitch.* Pull thread through next to the starting point. Place the needle back in beside the starting point and bring the point up a slight distance forward wrapping the thread around the needle.

CHAPTER TWO

BASIC QUILTING TECHNIQUES

The Quilt Top

Once you have decided how you want all the squares of your quilt to come together, stitch the blocks, dividers, and borders together to form the quilt top. Make sure that the seams match perfectly where they join. If you wish, you can sign and date your quilt at this point. Use embroidery thread or permanent pen.

Take care when marking the quilt top for the quilting stitches. The stitches will not cover these marks, so be sure that they are very light or removable. Use the same tracing process as for the appliqué. Water soluble pens are the best for marking the quilt. Be sure to use them as directed and to test them first on all fabrics. Lay the assembled quilt top face down on a smooth surface. Lay the batting on top of the backside of the quilt top. I use low loft batting—it's easier to quilt through. You may use high loft batting if you want a high relief to your design. Be sure to smooth out any folds or lumps as you go along. Finally, lay your backing fabric on top, right side up.

Basting

When basting the layers together, start from the center and work your way out to the sides. Baste all layers together using large, even stitches. The basting rows should be 4–6 inches apart and form a grid (Fig. 2-1).

Quilting

The needles you should use for quilting are called "betweens," sizes 8 or 9. Use extra strong

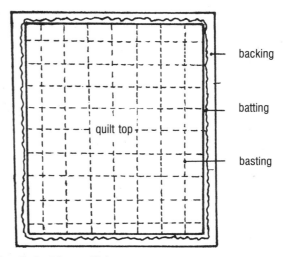

Fig. 2-1. The quilt top.

quilting thread. Pull the thread through beeswax to prevent tangling. Tie a small knot ½ inch from the end. The thread can match the fabric or it can be contrasting depending on the look you want. Place the quilt in a hoop or frame and begin in the middle.

Start stitching from inside the quilt and work the needle and thread towards you, outward, from right to left. Each time you start a new piece of thread, place the needle into the top layer ½ inch from where you want to begin. Catch some batting and push the needle back through the top where stitching is to begin. Give a slight tug to pull the knot inside, then take a small backstitch to secure the thread.

Use small, evenly spaced running stitches. Push the needle with a thimble placed on the middle finger of your top hand and press down the fabric in front of the needle with your thumb. Use the middle finger of the hand underneath the quilt to redirect the needle back to the top of the quilt. Try to get a rhythm going. When you reach the end of the thread, backstitch and bring the needle out. Tie a small knot and insert the needle back through the same hole. Pass the needle under the fabric about a ½ inch away. Bring the needle out, pulling the knot in, and trim any excess thread. After the quilting is complete, carefully trim away the excess batting and backing.

Binding

You can use a commercial binding or make your own. There are two types of binding; straight of grain and bias. Which type and width you use is a matter of taste. A 2½ to 3 inch wide binding finishes to a ½ inch, which is fairly standard and quite nice.

First baste around the edge of the quilt, then cut a strip of binding the length of the quilt plus 1 inch. If you are using a bias binding, you may need to attach a few strips together to get the length you need.

Fold the binding strips in half lengthwise, wrong sides together. Then fold the outside edges into the center. The width from the edge to the fold should be ½ inch. Pin the binding to the right side of the quilt (Fig. 2-2). Blindstitch along the length of the binding, using a thread color that matches the binding. Make sure you are sewing through all three layers. Wrap the remaining edge of the binding over the edge of the quilt. Tuck in the ½ inch seam allowance, pin it to the back of the quilt, and blindstitch.

When both sides of the quilt are finished, trim off the excess binding. Then bind the other two sides of the quilt the same way. Fold the ends under ½ inch and whip-stitch them closed.

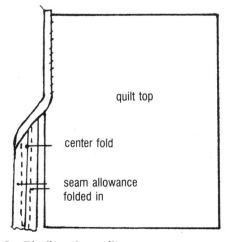

Fig. 2-2. Binding the quilt.

Cutting and Layout

I have included cutting and layout instructions for those who wish to make the quilts shown in this book. The templates and symbols I used are indicated on Figs. 2-3 and 2-4, though you may want to choose your own.

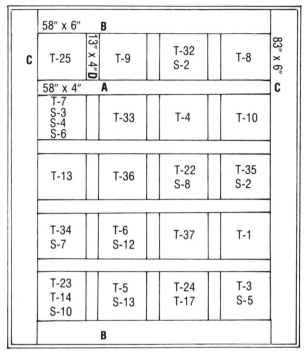

T = Template
S = Symbol

Fig. 2-3. Layout diagram for blue quilt (see color section).

Materials

(Width for all fabric is 44/45". A ½ inch seam allowance is included in all measurements. Quilt finishes to 82" × 67".)

2¾ yards of fabric for borders and latticework
2⅔ yards of fabric for squares
4⅔ yards of fabric for backing
Low loft batting, 84" × 68"

Cut the borders and strips for the latticework as shown in Fig. 2-5. There should be enough fabric left over for the straight-of-grain binding.

Cut twenty-one 13-inch squares, three across and seven down. You will only need twenty squares for the quilt, so you will have one left over.

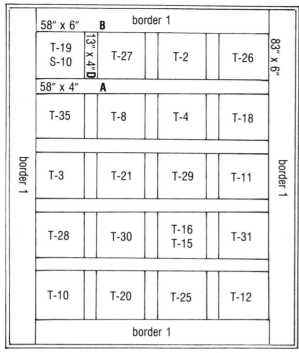

T = Template
S = Symbol

Fig. 2-4. Layout diagram for red quilt (see cover).

For the backing, cut the yardage into two 83-inch pieces, then sew them together along the length. Once the quilt is laid out, you'll have to trim the backing.

Hanging Quilts

You can hang your quilt by attaching a sleeve and inserting a dowel rod. To determine the length of the sleeve, measure the top of the quilt and add a 1 inch seam allowance. The width should be approximately 9" for a bed quilt and 7" for a wall hanging.

Hem the sleeve so it fits just inside the side bindings. Fold the strip right side together in half lengthwise and stitch along the seam allowance. Turn right side out and press. Place the sleeve just under the binding at the top of the quilt and line stitch across the top of the sleeve.

Now place the rod through the sleeve, making sure the fabric against the quilt is lying flat and not bulging around the rod. Pin the bottom of the sleeve to the quilt, pull the rod out, and blind stitch (see Fig. 1-6) the sides and bottom to the quilt. Replace the rod and hang the quilt.

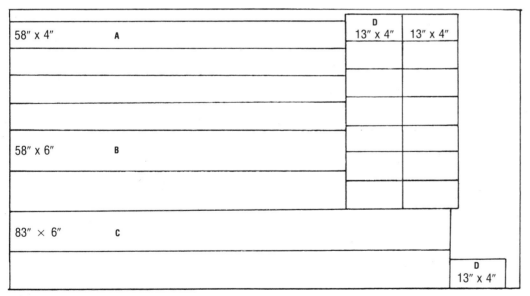

Fig. 2-5. Cutting diagram for quilt.

CHAPTER THREE

DECORATING ACCESSORIES

Pillows

Pillows are easy to construct and fun to design. You can use different fabrics for the top and bottom pieces. If you decide to use a border, you can use a third fabric for that. See the color section for pillow ideas.

Materials

Paper for pattern and templates
½ yard of fabric for a 13″ × 16″ square pillow or a 13″ round pillow
½ yard for border (optional)
3¼ yards of lace for trim (optional)
Remnants for cats and symbols
Matching thread
Polyfill for stuffing

Directions

1. Decide what size and shape you want the pillow to be and draw the shape on a piece of paper. If you would like a border, measure in from the outer edge of the paper and draw the width you want. Don't forget to add seam allowances where needed.

2. Choose your cat template and symbols. Sketch them onto the paper pattern. You now have your design.

3. Lay the fabric over the pattern to cut the top piece, including the seam allowance but not the border.

4. Cut the templates and symbols from the appliqué fabric and appliqué to the top piece.

5. Cut the borders (be sure to include seam allowances) and sew them to the top piece, adding on the pieces that will overlap last (see Fig. 3-1).

Fig. 3-1. Adding borders to pillows.

6. Cut the backing to the same dimensions as the top piece (including the borders, if any).

Note: To add a lace trim or ruffle, see Chapter One for instructions.

7. Place the right sides of the top and bottom piece together and stitch around the entire pillow. Leave enough of an opening to turn and stuff.

8. Turn right sides out, press, and stuff with polyfill. Hand stitch the opening closed.

Fig. 3-2.

Fig. 3-4.

Fig. 3-3.

Figs. 3-2—3-4. These are just a few examples of the different types of pillows you can make.

Curtains

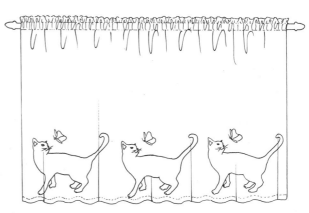

Fig. 3-5. Idea for curtains using template 35 and symbol 2.

To make a curtain, measure the width of your window and double it to give the curtain gathers when hung. Measure the height and add extra for the top ruffle and finishing. Although it's a matter of taste, use Fig. 3-6 to help determine the amount of ruffle and fabric needed.

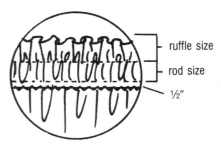

ruffle size
rod size
½"

Fig. 3-6. Top ruffle.

For example, for a 2 inch ruffle add 2 inches then a little more than ½ the rod circumference and ½ inch seam allowance to the height. Zigzag the top raw edge. Fold back the amount that you just added, then stitch a line 2 inches from the fold. This is the ruffle. Then stitch another line the distance that you allowed for the rod circumference. This is the rod pocket. You will have a ½ inch seam allowance left over already finished with the zigzag stitch. For a 1 inch hem, add an extra 1¼ inches, turn ¼ inch under and hem at 1 inch (Fig. 3-7).

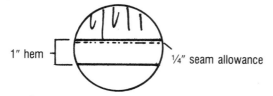

Fig. 3-7. Hem.

Sewing Machine Cover

(A ½ inch seam allowance is included in all measurements.)

Materials

¾ yard fabric
2½ yards piping
Matching thread
Remnants for cat (I used template 26)
Embroidery thread for details

Directions

1. Cut the fabric (see Fig. 3-8).

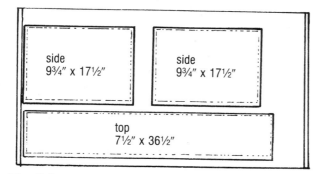

Fig. 3-8. Cutting diagram for sewing machine cover.

2. Appliqué the cat of your choice onto the right side of one side piece (Fig. 3-9a).

Fig. 3-9. Sewing machine cover.

3. You may want to buy piping and sew it onto the right side of both side pieces by matching its raw edges to your fabrics. The corner will be slightly curved (clipping the piping seam allowance at the curve will help).

4. Sew both side pieces to each side of the top by placing the right sides together and aligning the raw edges (Fig. 3-9b). Use a zipper foot to sew as close to the piping as possible. Turn right side out and hem (Fig. 3-9c). See the color section for the finished project.

Cat Basket Pillow Sham

This is a simple project that should take about three hours. You can choose a fabric that will match the decor of the room you plan to put the basket in (see Fig. 3-10).

Fig. 3-10. Cat basket pillow sham.

Materials

(makes a sham for a 12″ × 18″ pillow)

Paper for templates and pattern
1 yard of fabric for sham with ruffle
½ yard of fabric for ruffle
¾ yard of fabric for sham without ruffle
Matching thread
Remnants for cat templates (I used template 13, which requires a 6″ × 10″ remnant)
Embroidery thread for eyes and nose

Directions

1. Trace the pillow you are making the sham for on paper. You will need to adjust the yardages if your pillow is larger than 12″ × 18″. See Fig. 3-12 for the cutting diagram.

2. To make the pillow top pattern (A), add an extra 1″ around the outline for height and seam allowance. Cut out pattern A twice.

3. Take one pattern A and fold in half. Measure 4″ from the fold line, draw a line from top to bottom, and cut along the line (see Fig. 3-11). This will be the pillow bottom pattern (B).

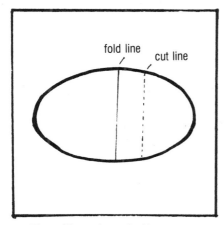

Fig. 3-11. The pillow sham bottom.

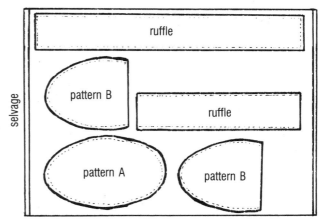

Fig. 3-12. Cutting diagram for cat basket pillow sham.

4. For the ruffle, cut 8″ wide strips, the length of which should equal that of the circumference doubled. The width includes the seam allowances (see Chapter One for instructions).

5. Cut one pattern A out of the fabric and appliqué the desired templates and symbols.

6. Cut two pieces of pattern B from the fabric and hem ¼″ along the straight line. Fold again, turning the straight line under 1½″. Iron the fold. Do this for both pieces.

7. Place each piece of fabric B, right side down, against the right side of fabric A. The two B pieces should overlap approximately 3″. Pin or baste in place.

Note: If adding a ruffle, make sure it is placed between the two B pieces.

8. Sew around the entire sham. Turn right side out. Trim the excess threads and slip your pillow in (see color section for finished project).

Ideas

The projects in this chapter are just a few of the many items you can make for your home or to give as gifts. A wall hanging is a wonderful way to remember your favorite pet or to celebrate the birth of kittens (Figs. 3-13 and 3-14). If you don't want to make a quilt, you can buy a bedspread and appliqué cats onto it. Create your own de-

Fig. 3-13. Memorial wall hanging.

signer bed sets, for adults and children, by appliquéing onto sheets, pillow cases, and blankets.

Fig. 3-14. Wall hanging to celebrate the birth of your kittens.

Couch and chair covers can also be appliquéd. Use the templates to make stencils and decorate walls, furniture, and cabinets. Doilies, bird cage covers, and heating pad covers can be appliquéd, embroidered, or stenciled.

CHAPTER FOUR

KITCHEN KITTIES

Tablecloth

Tablecloth ideas are endless—here are just two. Use your imagination and have fun. Think of what you can do for gifts and the holidays!

Fig. 4-1. Tablecloth project.

Materials

Fabric for tablecloth
1 yard of fabric for the templates
Embroidery thread for details

Directions

1. Choose your fabric. I find it's easiest to purchase 45" or 60" fabric (depending on the size of the table) and ask the clerk to square it. This way you will not have a seam. If your table is rectangular, measure the length and width and add enough to all four sides to achieve the amount of drape you want.

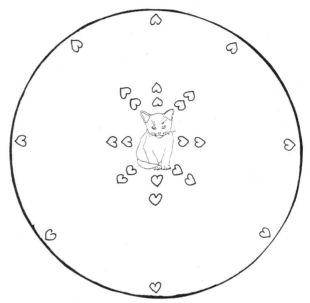

Fig. 4-2. Tablecloth idea using template 24 and symbol 28.

2. Use woven fabrics. Poly cotton is good because you will have less wrinkling and it's easy to wash.

3. Appliqué the designs you have chosen (for the cloth in Fig. 4-1, I used templates 27, 28, 32, and 36) and hem. See the color section for the finished project.

Note: To prevent staining, use a commercial stain repellent, such as Scotch Guard, on the finished cloth.

Place Mat

(A ½ inch seam allowance is included in all measurements.)

Fig. 4-3. Place mat.

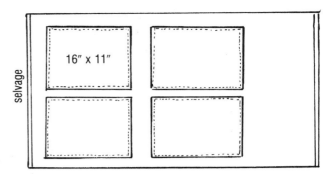

Fig. 4-5. Cutting diagram for place mat tops.

Materials

(makes four place mats)

Paper for pattern
1 yard of fabric for 4 top squares
1½ yards of fabric for backs and borders
Remnants for cats and symbols
Matching thread

Directions

1. Cut fabric (see Figs. 4-4 and 4-5).

2. Appliqué the cat of your choice onto the 16″ × 11″ center squares (I used template 30).

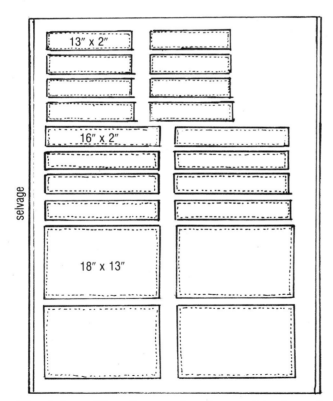

Fig. 4-4. Cutting diagram for place mat backs and borders.

3. Add the borders: Sew two 16″ × 2″ strips to the top and bottom of each center square, right sides together and raw edges aligned. Then sew two 13″ × 2″ strips to the sides in the same manner.

4. Position the back piece over the place mat top, right sides together, and stitch around the entire place mat. Leave an opening only wide enough to turn.

5. Turn inside out, press, stitch up the opening, then top stitch as shown in Fig. 4-3. Place mats finish to 17″ × 12″. See finished project in color section.

Tea Cozy

This charming and practical tea cozy is easy to make and fun to use. For a nice finishing touch, I added a ruffle. To do this, follow steps 1 through 4. Measure the arc of one of the pieces and double it to determine the length. Width should be 3½″. Fold the fabric in half lengthwise (right sides together), single stitch the ends closed, and turn right side out, which will fold fabric in half lengthwise.

With right sides out, press the fold then sew raw edges together with a long single stitch. Pull the top thread while pushing the fabric inward and gather to fit the arch. Next place the ruffle in the seam by putting the raw edges together. The ruffle will face into the cozy. Baste in place. Position the back over the front with the ruffle in between (Fig. 4-6c).

Materials

Paper for drawing pattern
½ yard of calico for cozy
7″ × 10″ piece of fabric for appliqué
½ yard of low loft batting
Fabric for ruffle

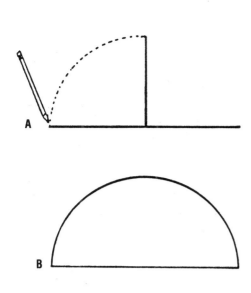

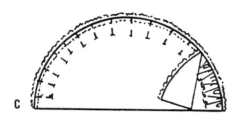

Fig. 4-6. Tea cozy.

Directions

1. Cut the fabric (see Fig. 4-7).

2. Create the pattern for the cozy by drawing a line 15″ long on a piece of paper. From the center of the line, draw a perpendicular line 10″ high. Connect the vertical line to the ends

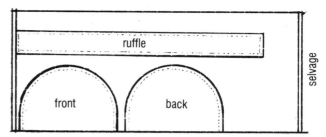

Fig. 4-7. Cutting diagram for tea cozy.

of the horizontal line by drawing an arc (Fig. 4-6a).

3. On folded fabric, place the straight edge of the pattern on the fold and cut around the arc (Fig. 4-6b). Do this twice to get the front and back pieces. Place the pattern on a single layer of the batting and cut two semi-circular pieces.

4. Open one piece of the fabric and appliqué the cat of your choice onto the right side of the top half (I used template 3 and symbol 5).

5. Place the batting on the wrong side of the fabric and fold the fabric over so that all three curved sides are together. Do this for both pieces of fabric. Then place the front and back together.

6. Sew all layers together at the arc. Turn cozy right side out. See finished project (Fig. 4-6d) in color section.

Ideas

You can create an entire kitchen of kittens easily and inexpensively. Appliqué onto dish towels and pot holders (see color section) as well as aprons, napkins, place mats, and tablecloths. Appliance covers can be made for toaster ovens, mixers, toasters, etc. (follow the general instructions for the sewing machine cover in chapter three and adapt the dimensions to your appliance). Remember, you can either make these items yourself or buy them and do your own appliquéing.

CHAPTER FIVE

PURR-FECT HOLIDAYS

Christmas Tree Skirt

This "cut and glue" tree skirt can be made in about 60 minutes for as little as $16.00. The directions below are for the skirt shown in the color section. Feel free to use whatever color combinations and templates you desire. For a variation, use fabrics instead of felt and hem the skirt. Cats and ornaments can be appliquéd onto the skirt.

Fig. 5-1. Christmas tree skirt.

Materials

Several pieces of newspaper or large sheets of paper taped together to form a square approximately 45" × 45"

Thick string

1¼ yards of red or green felt for skirt
¾ yards of black felt for cats
Several remnants of different colored felt for ornaments, including some pink for the ears
Appliqué thread
Glitter paint, sequins, or other festive embellishments

Directions

1. To create the pattern for the skirt, tie a pen to the string, then measure and cut the string at 20". Pin the end of the string to the center of the paper. Place a small piece of cardboard under the paper and tape it to the work surface. The cardboard will help secure the pin. Rotate the string like a compass to draw a circle 40" in diameter. Cut the string to 2½" from the pen, pin to the center of the paper, and draw a circle 5" in diameter.

2. Using a pinking shears, cut the fabric from the pattern. After cutting the center hole, cut a straight line from the center to the outer edge.

3. Choose the templates you want to use and make appliqués out of the black felt (I used templates 34, 14, 15, and 17, and symbols 18 and 20). Embroider details and glue on appliqués for eyes, nose, and ears, if desired. Cut the symbols from the colored felt.

Note: I enlarged the cat templates by about 44%. This can be done easily at most copy shops.

4. Decide how you want to arrange the cats and ornaments **before** glueing them to the skirt. Ornaments can be "strung together" with embroidery, glitter paint, or a combination of both. See color section for finished project.

Note: You may use cotton, poly cotton, or velvet instead of felt. Most woven fabrics will work. Machine or hand appliqué your design and hem around the curved edge.

Christmas Stocking

Fig. 5-2. Stocking idea using template 19 and symbol 29 (star). To create the holiday package shown, sew or glue ribbon over a square, attach to the stocking, and finish with symbol 5 (bow).

Enjoy the holiday season with a festive Christmas stocking made from either felt, a woven cotton, poly cotton, or velvet. You can make the pattern by tracing a stocking or drawing one free hand. I chose felt for my stocking and used template 24 and symbol 20.

Fig. 5-3. Holiday stocking project showing dimensions.

Materials

Paper for pattern
½ yard of felt or a woven fabric
½ yard of lining
4″ of ribbon for the loop

Several remnants for the templates and symbols
Sequins, glitter paint, and other festive embellishments

Directions (for felt)

1. Place the pattern on the fabric and cut two pieces to the exact size you want the stocking to be. Do not add a seam allowance.

Note: I did not use a lining for the felt stocking.

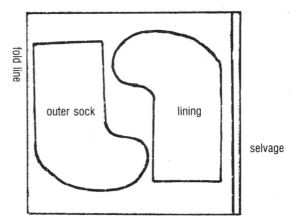

Fig. 5-4. Cutting diagram for stocking.

2. Appliqué, glue, or paint the design onto the right side of the top piece. Make sure the toe of the stocking is facing in the direction you want.

3. Sew the stocking pieces right sides out with a zigzag stitch, leaving the top open.

4. Sew on a 2″ ribbon to hang the stocking.

Directions (for woven fabric)

1. Add a ½″ seam allowance all the way around the stocking on the paper pattern.

2. Fold the fabric (right sides together), place the pattern on it, and cut two pieces (Fig. 5-4). Do the same with the lining fabric.

Note: The lining can be the same fabric as the stocking provided it is thin. If you are using velvet, you will need a thin lining fabric.

3. Appliqué, glue, or paint the design onto the right side of the top piece. Make sure the toe of the stocking is facing in the direction you want.

Note: If you are using velvet, you will have to sew your design on.

4. Sew the stocking pieces right sides together, leaving the top open. Do the same for the lining pieces.

5. On the outer stocking, stitch a 2″ loop of ribbon at the seam, facing down, with the ends going over the seam allowance. This will be used to hang the stocking.

6. Turn the outer stocking inside out and place the lining (facing in the same direction) inside the outer stocking with right sides together. Make sure the loop is down (Fig. 5-5a).

7. Stitch around the top, leaving a small opening to turn them right side out (Fig. 5-5b).

8. Turn and press and tuck the lining back inside, this time with the right sides out. Baste the small opening closed (Fig. 5-5c).

Ideas

Brighten up your holiday table with appliquéd place mats, napkins, and a tablecloth.

A handmade gift is always cherished. What better way to surprise your favorite cat lover than with a framed wall hanging? Choose a template that best characterizes his or her cat and surround it with festive holly berries and leaves (Fig. 5-6).

Children and animals just seem to go together, especially at Christmas. How about a crib quilt or diaper bag with pastel kittens?

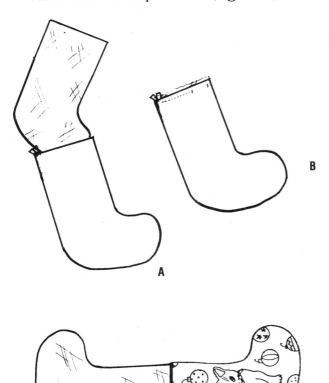

Fig. 5-5. Adding a lining to the stocking.

Fig. 5-6. Idea for holiday wall hanging using template 28 and symbol 19.

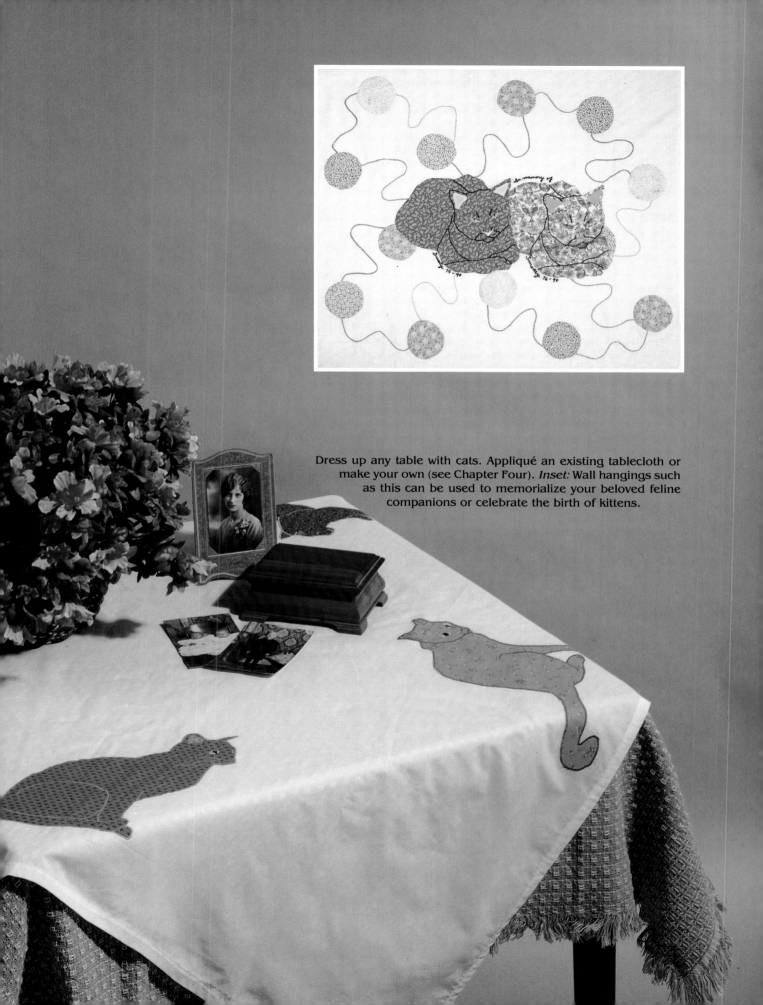

Dress up any table with cats. Appliqué an existing tablecloth or make your own (see Chapter Four). *Inset:* Wall hangings such as this can be used to memorialize your beloved feline companions or celebrate the birth of kittens.

Decorating Accessories (Chapter Three). *Top:* Keep appliances dust-free with creative cat covers such as this nifty sewing machine cover. *Bottom:* Pillows can be made in any shape and size (*left,* template 21; *right,* template 30). Add a ruffle for that special touch.

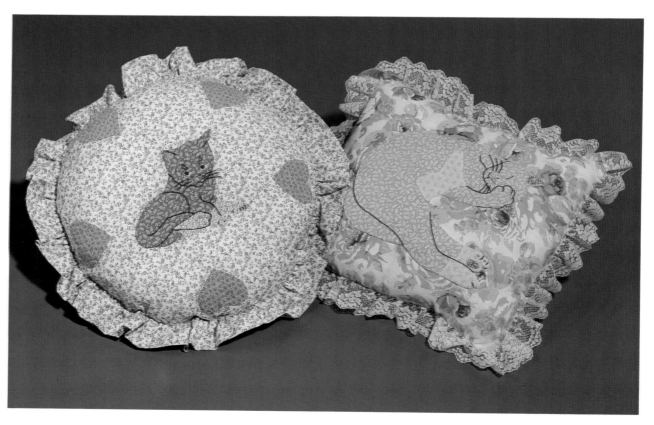

Accessorize a kitchen by appliquéing the cats of your choice onto pot holders, dish towels, napkins, and aprons. A quick way to make a personalized gift.

Custom design your own colorful quilt with the dozens of templates and symbols provided. (See Chapter Two for quilting techniques and layout diagrams.)

Top: Teatime with Tiddles. With the instructions provided in Chapter Four, you can make this enchanting cozy that will warm both your tea and your heart. *Bottom:* Decorating accessories, such as pillows, can be made quickly and inexpensively. Borders can be either lapped (as shown) or mitered. See Chapter Three for ideas and instructions. (*Left*, template 28; *right*, template 2.)

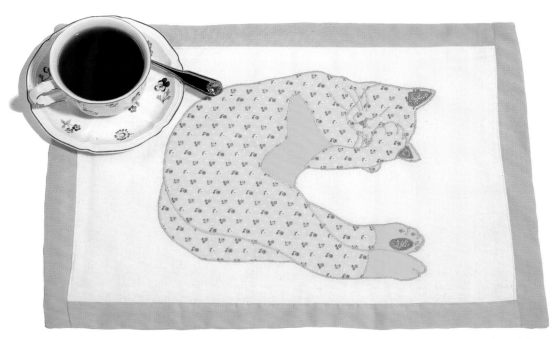

Top: This charming place mat (Chapter Four) can be used in the kitchen, dining room, or on a breakfast tray. *Bottom:* The possiblities for catty clothing are endless. Update an old wardrobe or embellish a new one with appliqués (template 2 shown). See Chapter Six for instructions and ideas.

Purr-fect Holidays (Chapter Five). Put cats under your Christmas tree. This cut-and-glue tree skirt is easy and fun to make. *Inset:* Make a stocking for your kitty, yourself, or anyone! An ideal holiday gift.

Give your cat a cozy bed to curl up on. This pillow sham (Chapter Three) can be designed to match the decor of any room in your house.

CATTY CLOTHING

T-shirts, Sweatshirts, and Dresses

Find yourself an old sweatshirt or T-shirt, or buy a new one, and appliqué the cat of your choice onto it. Add a bow, flowers, or ball of yarn—you get the idea.

Make a child's dress by taking a large T-shirt and adding a ruffle to the bottom (see Chapter One). Appliqué your favorite cat onto it and you have a cute designer dress.

Ideas

Almost any item of clothing can be appliquéd. If you don't make your own clothing, buy inexpensive garments and embellish them. Dress up an old wardrobe with perky kittens. Cover mends, stains, and threadbare spots with colorful appliqués. Compliment a new wardrobe with personalized accessories (scarves, shawls, handbags). Turn everyday garments into holiday outfits and back-to-school clothes.

Fig. 6-2. Sweatshirt using template 2.

Fig. 6-1. Idea for T-shirt using template 36 and symbol 5.

Fig. 6-3. Child's dress using template 15.

TEMPLATES, BORDERS, AND SYMBOLS

TEMPLATE 1

TEMPLATE 2

23

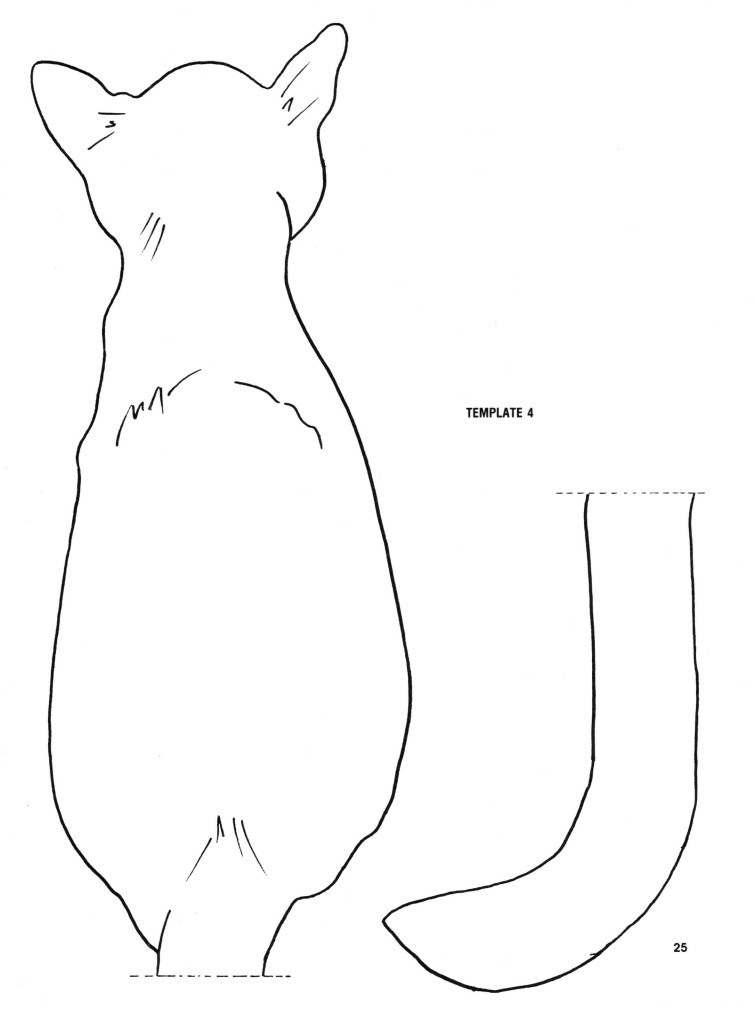

TEMPLATE 4

25

TEMPLATE 5

TEMPLATE 6

27

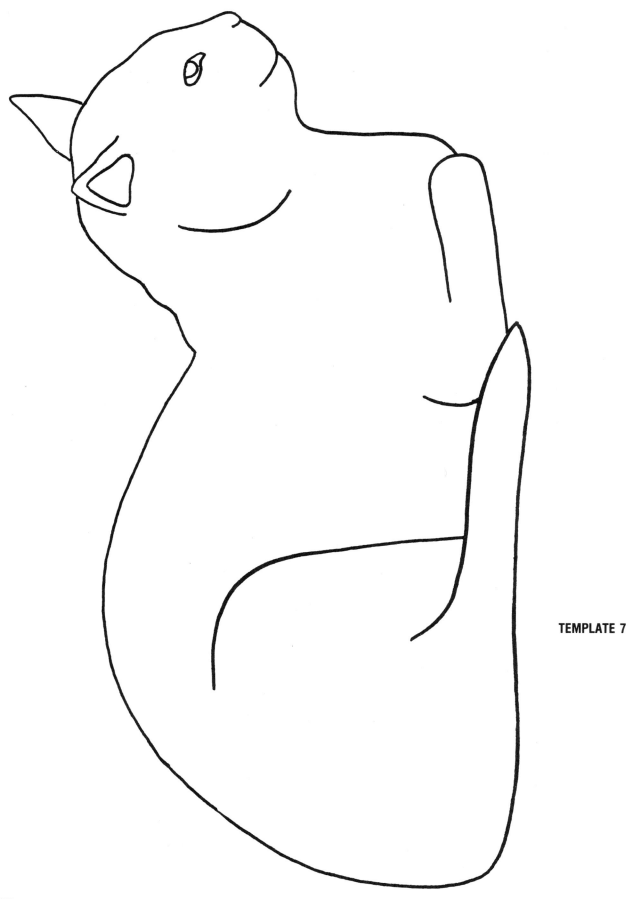

TEMPLATE 7

TEMPLATE 8

TEMPLATE 9

TEMPLATE 10

TEMPLATE 11

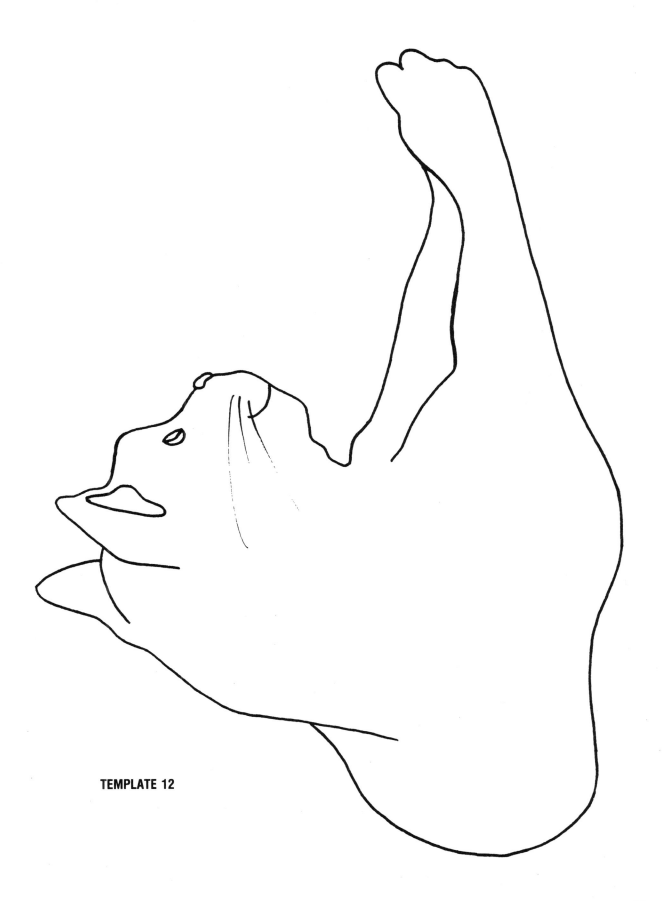

TEMPLATE 12

TEMPLATE 13

TEMPLATE 14

TEMPLATE 15

TEMPLATE 16

TEMPLATE 17

TEMPLATE 18

TEMPLATE 19

TEMPLATE 20

TEMPLATE 21

TEMPLATE 22

TEMPLATE 23

TEMPLATE 24

TEMPLATE 25 (1 of 2)

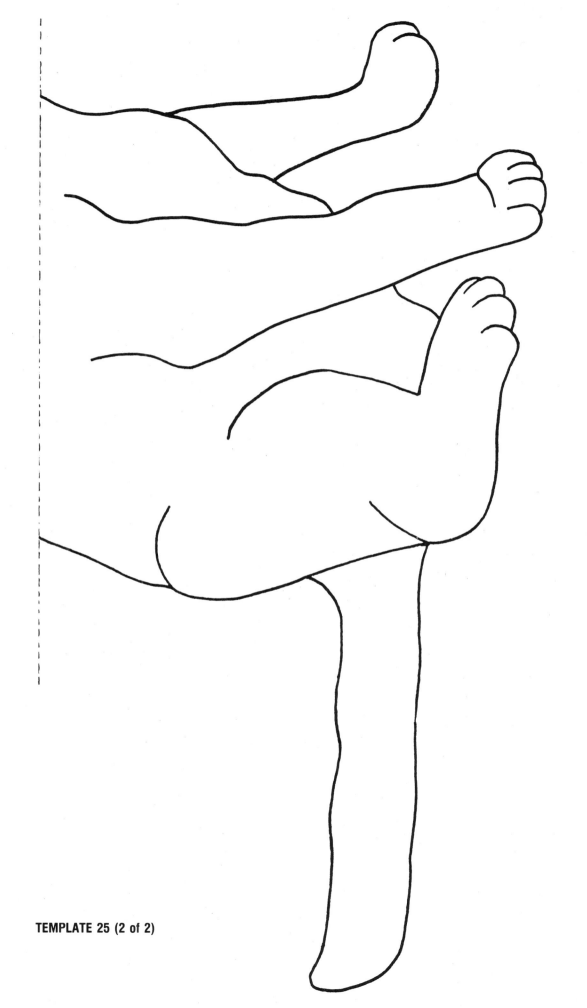

TEMPLATE 25 (2 of 2)

TEMPLATE 26 (1 of 2)

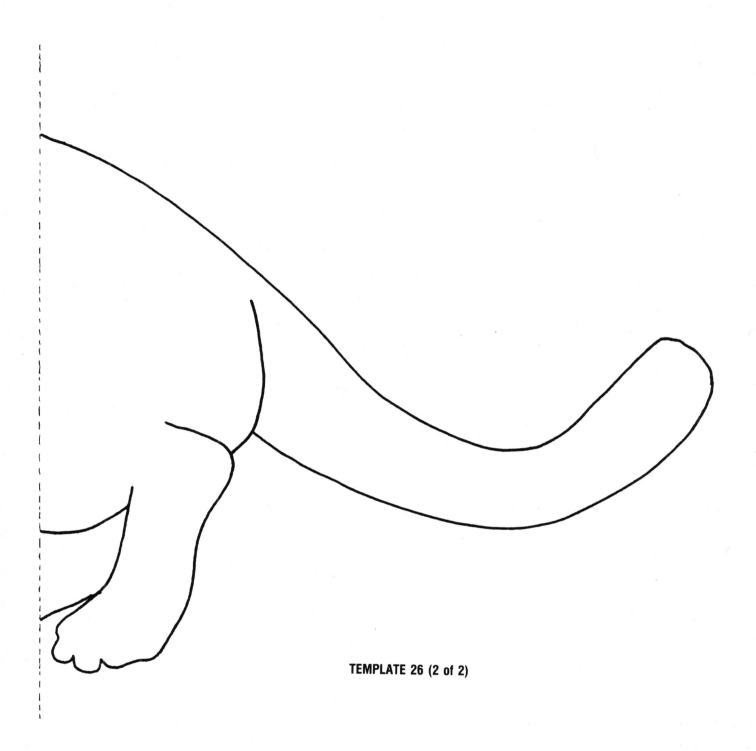

TEMPLATE 26 (2 of 2)

TEMPLATE 27 (1 of 2)

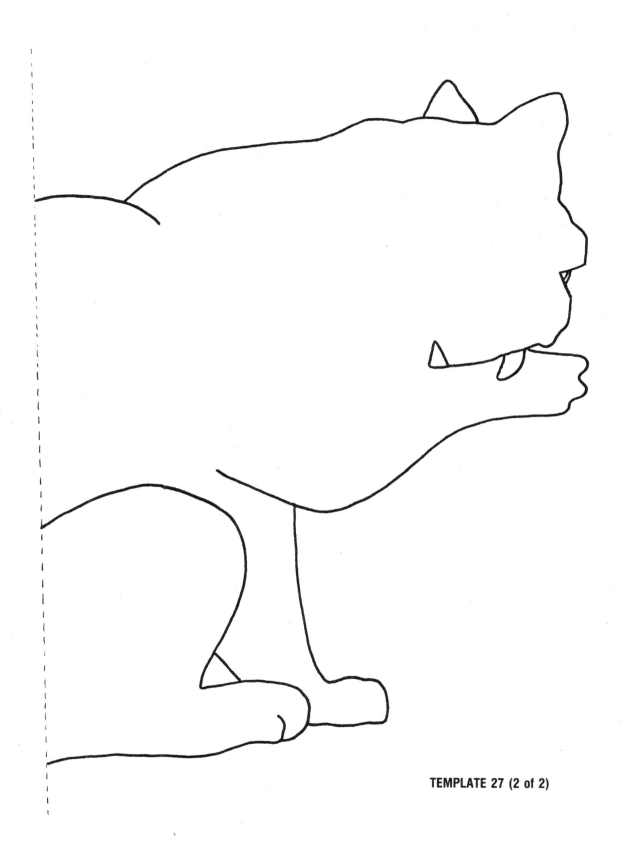

TEMPLATE 27 (2 of 2)

51

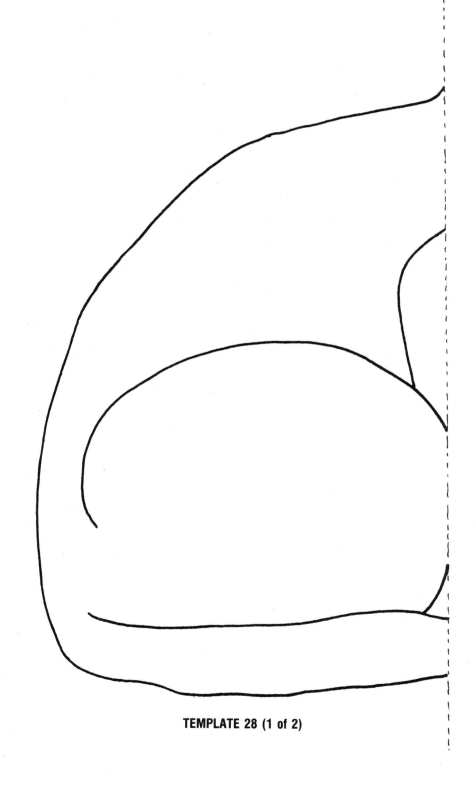

TEMPLATE 28 (1 of 2)

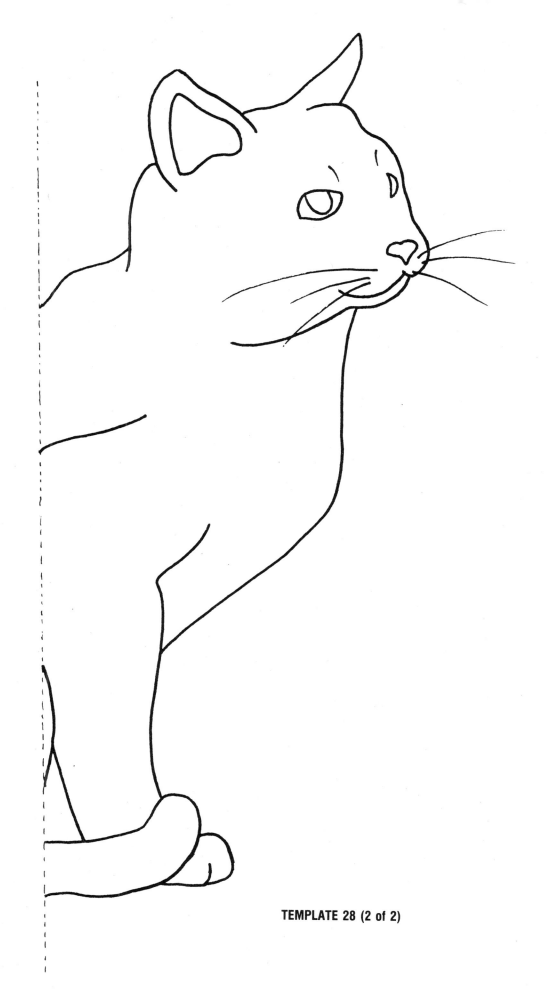

TEMPLATE 28 (2 of 2)

TEMPLATE 29 (1 of 2)

54

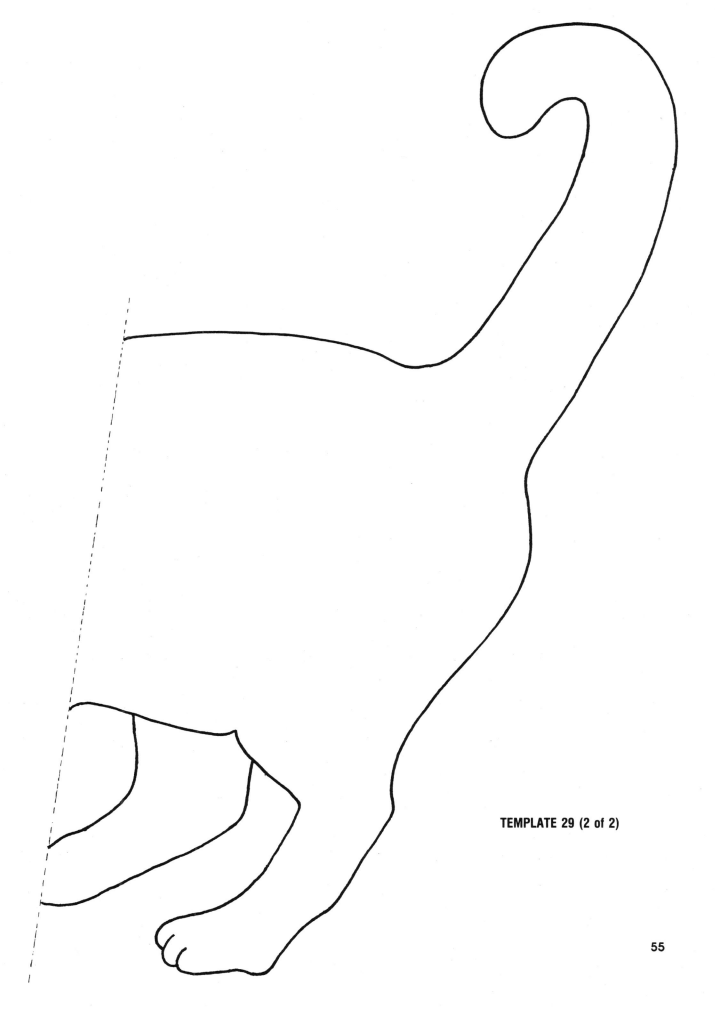

TEMPLATE 29 (2 of 2)

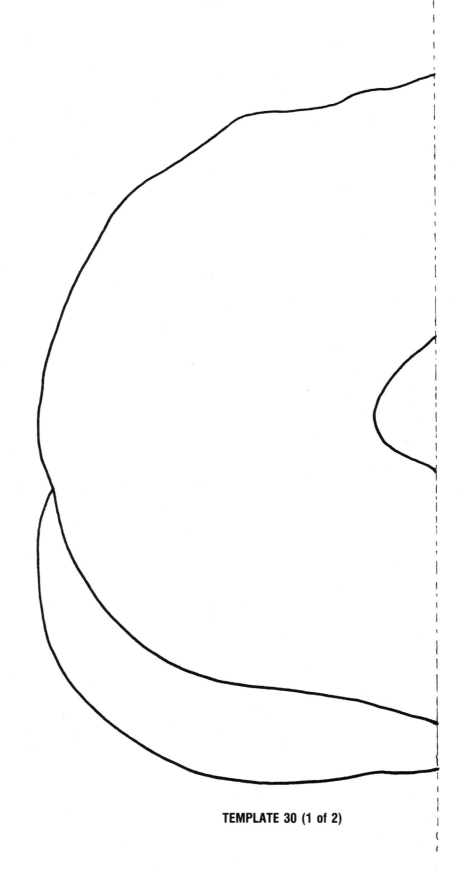

TEMPLATE 30 (1 of 2)

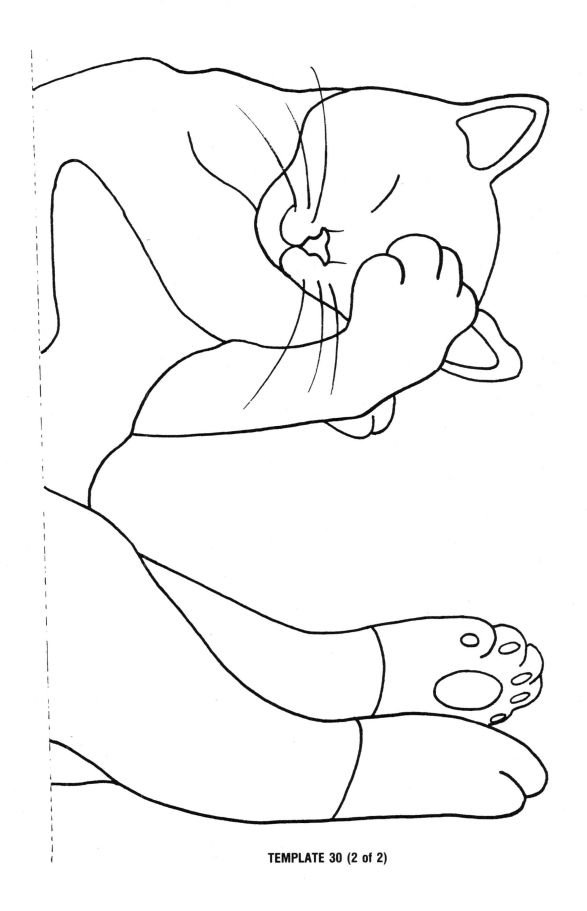

TEMPLATE 30 (2 of 2)

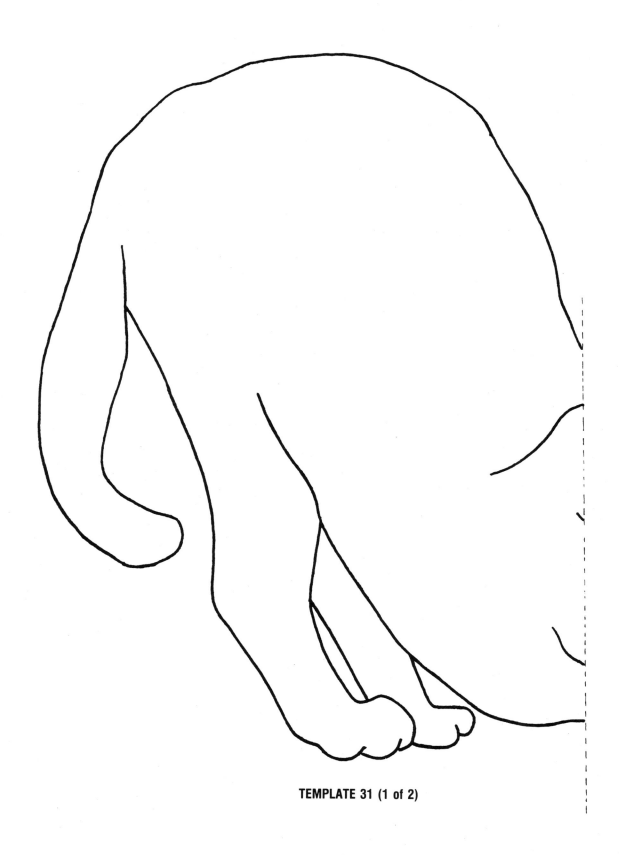

TEMPLATE 31 (1 of 2)

TEMPLATE 31 (2 of 2)

TEMPLATE 32 (1 of 2)

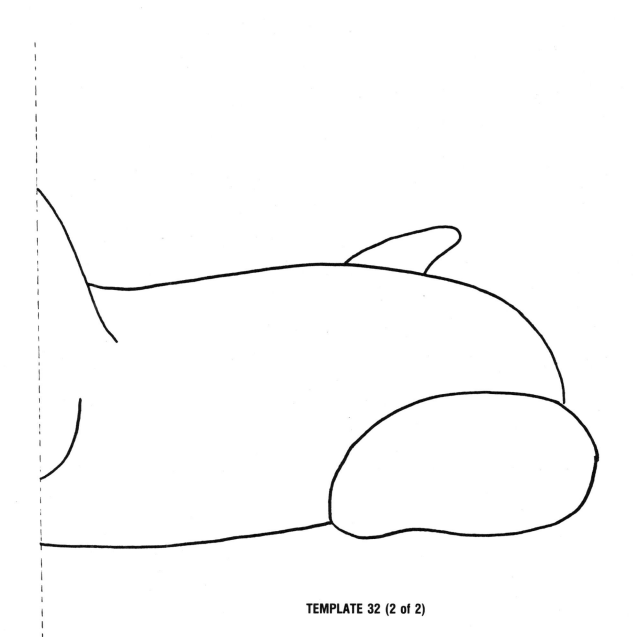

TEMPLATE 32 (2 of 2)

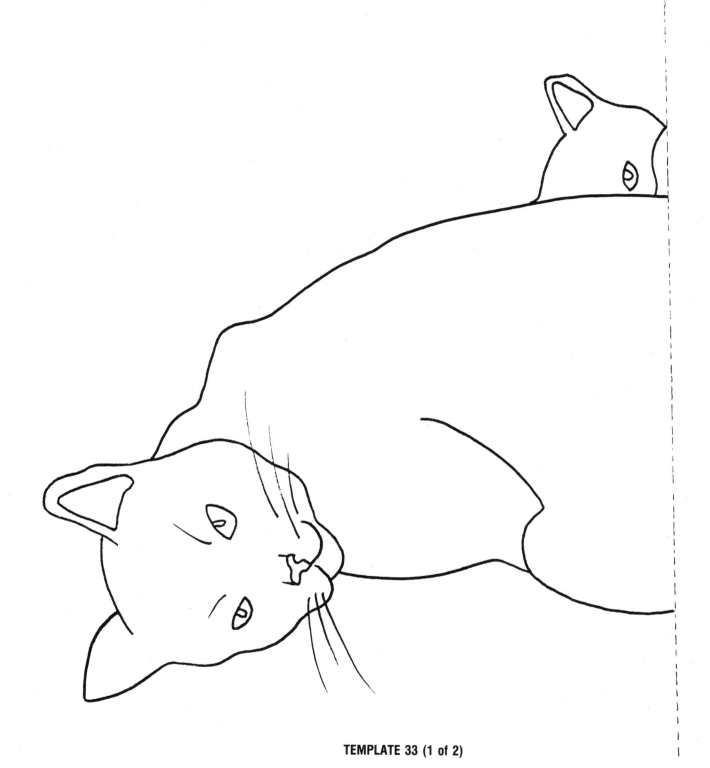

TEMPLATE 33 (1 of 2)

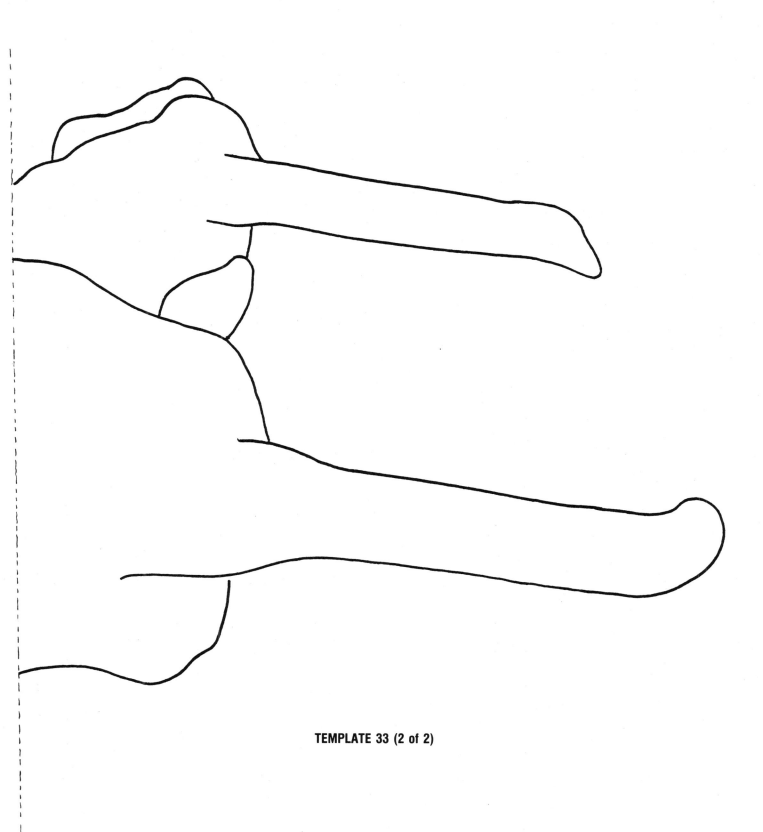

TEMPLATE 33 (2 of 2)

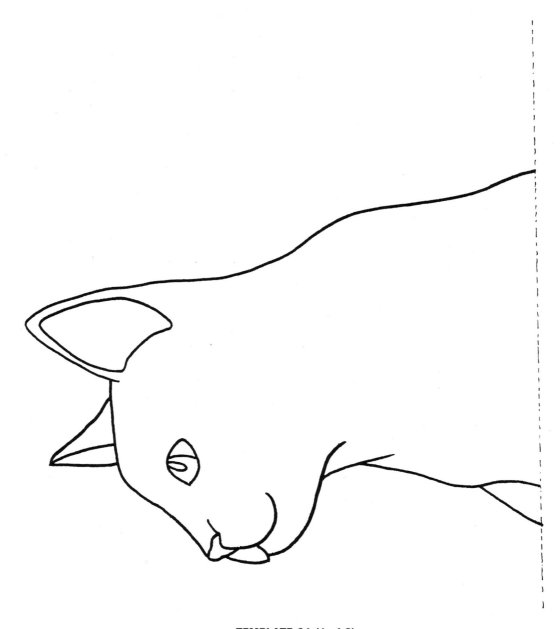

TEMPLATE 34 (1 of 2)

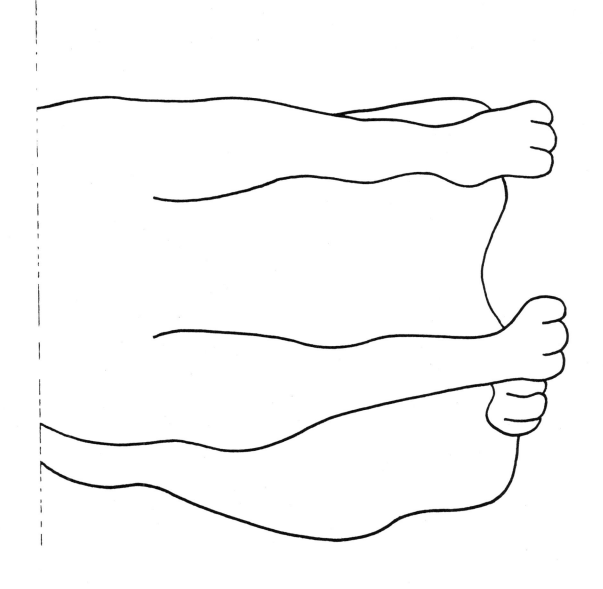

TEMPLATE 34 (2 of 2)

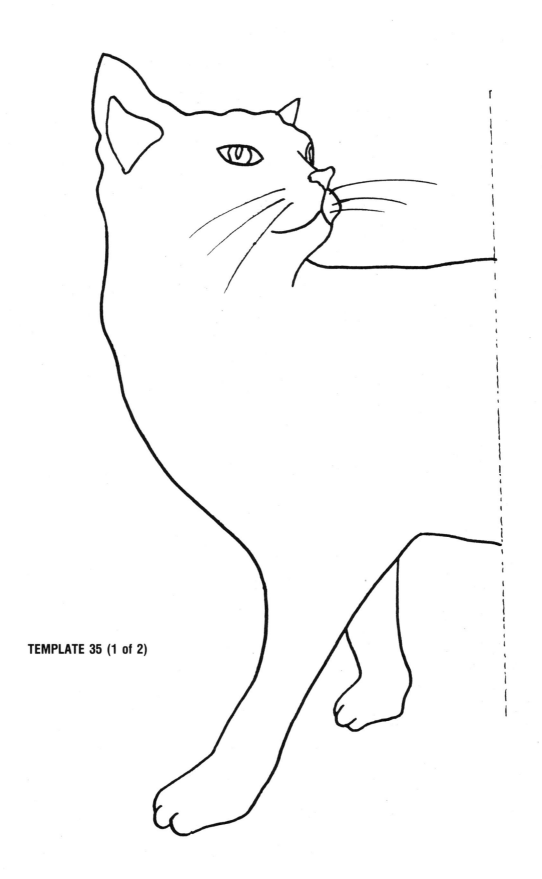

TEMPLATE 35 (1 of 2)

TEMPLATE 35 (2 of 2)

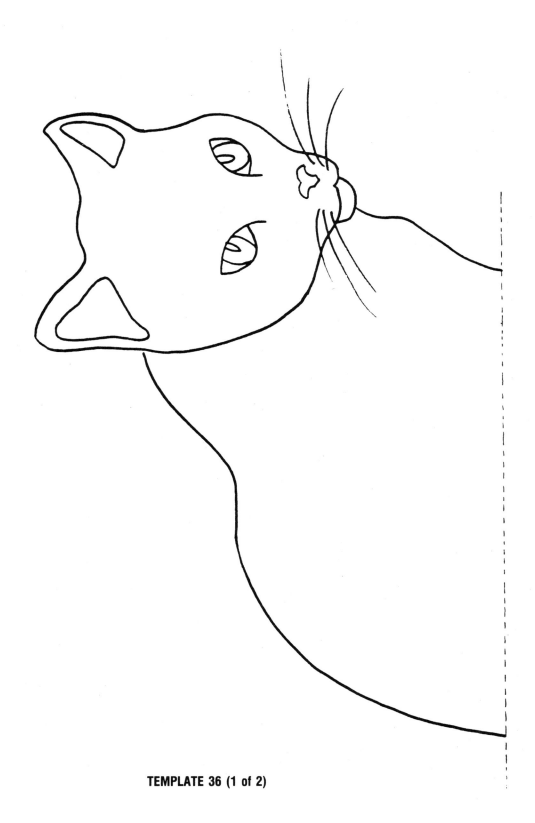

TEMPLATE 36 (1 of 2)

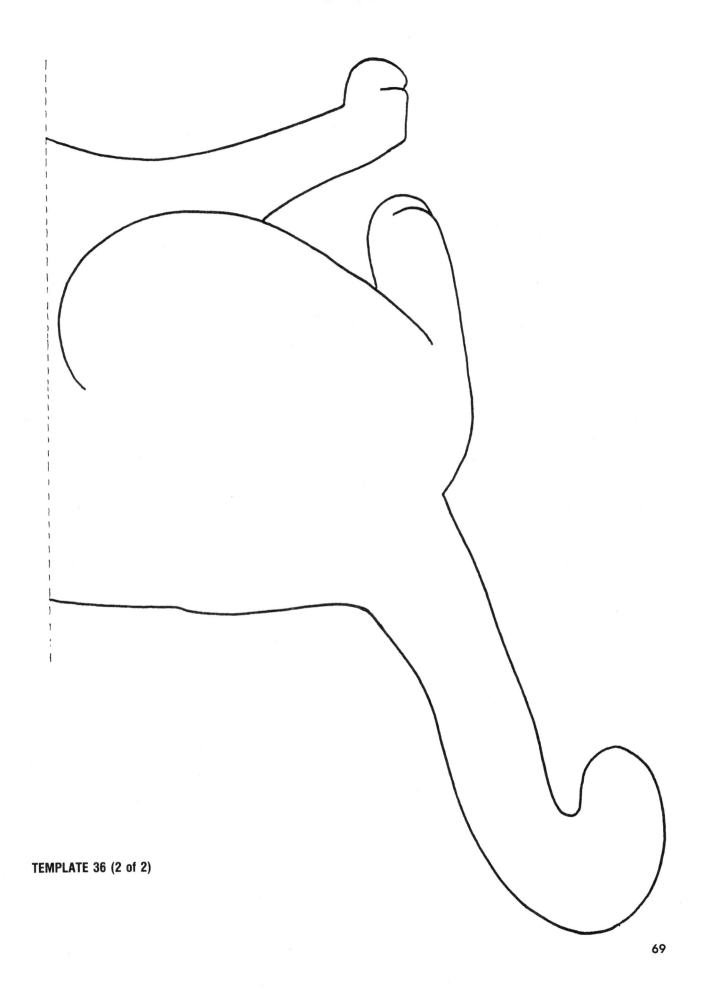

TEMPLATE 36 (2 of 2)

TEMPLATE 37 (1 of 2)

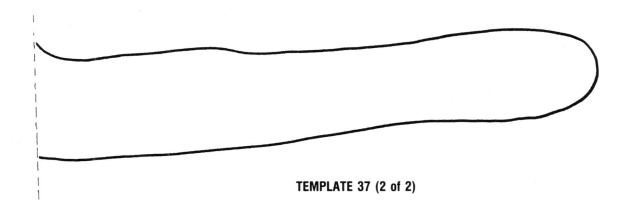

TEMPLATE 37 (2 of 2)

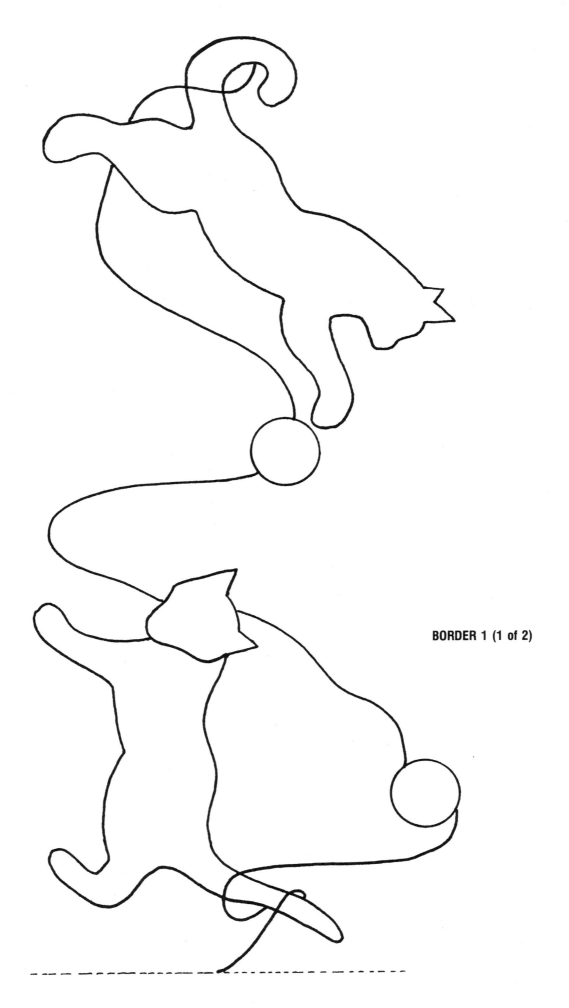

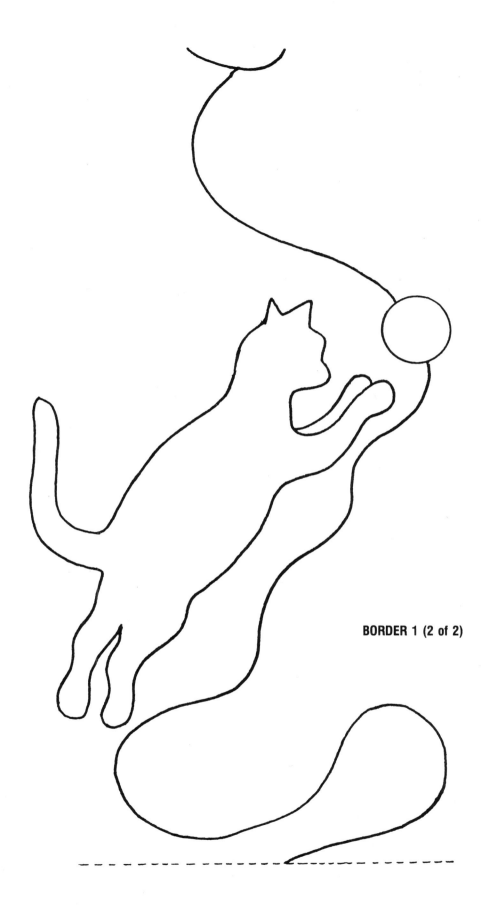

BORDER 1 (2 of 2)

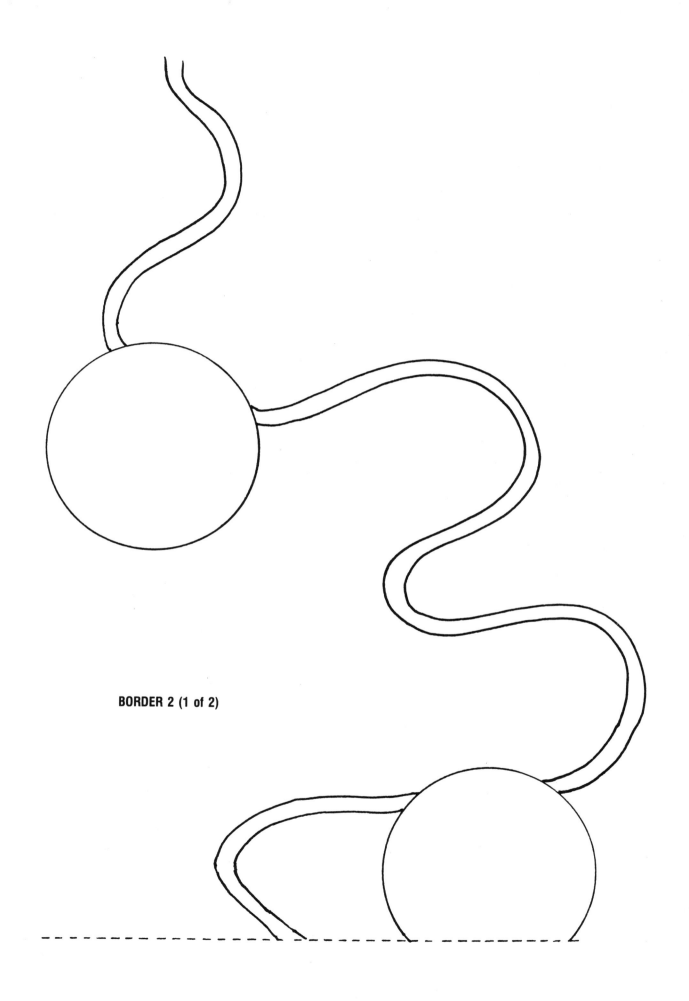

BORDER 2 (1 of 2)

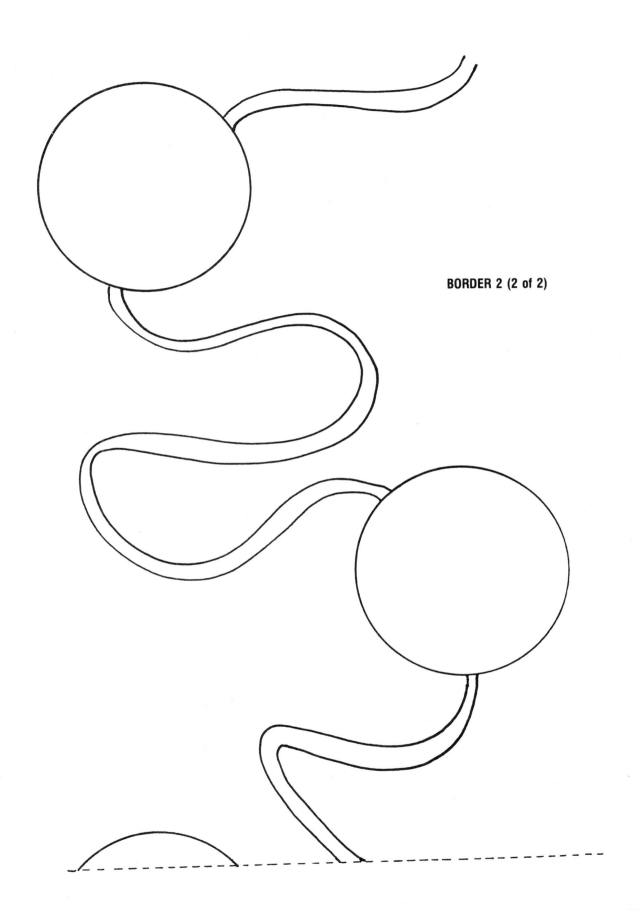

BORDER 2 (2 of 2)

Symbol 2

Symbol 3

Symbol 4

Symbol 5

Symbol 1

your cat's name

Symbol 6

Symbol 7

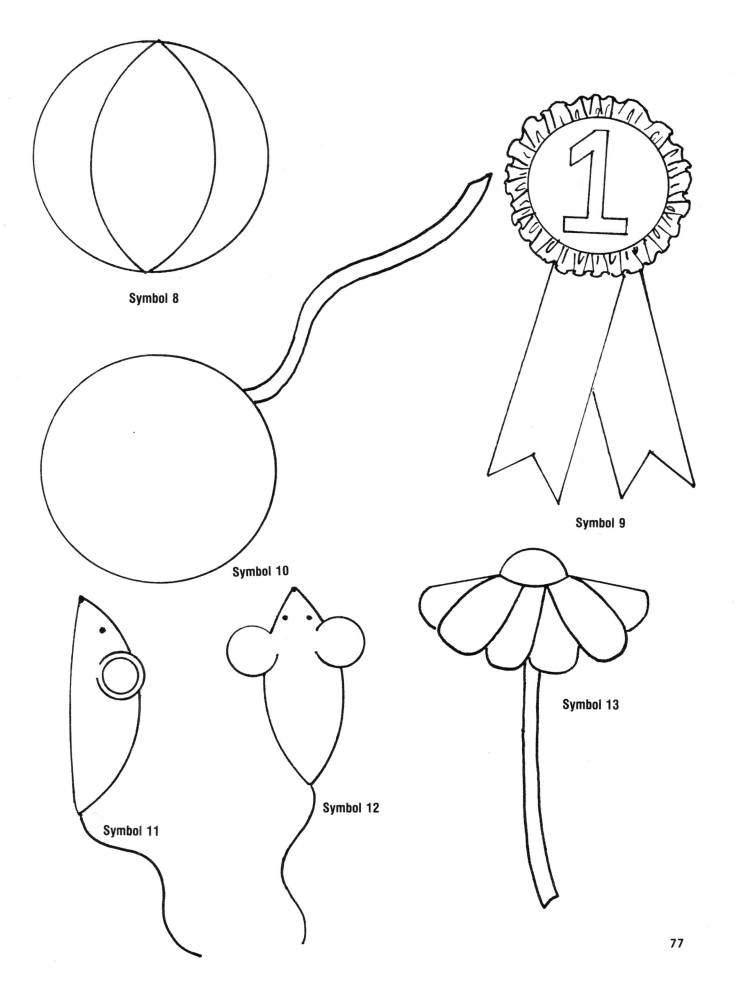

Symbol 8

Symbol 9

Symbol 10

Symbol 11

Symbol 12

Symbol 13

77

Symbol 14

Symbol 15

Symbol 16

Symbol 17

78

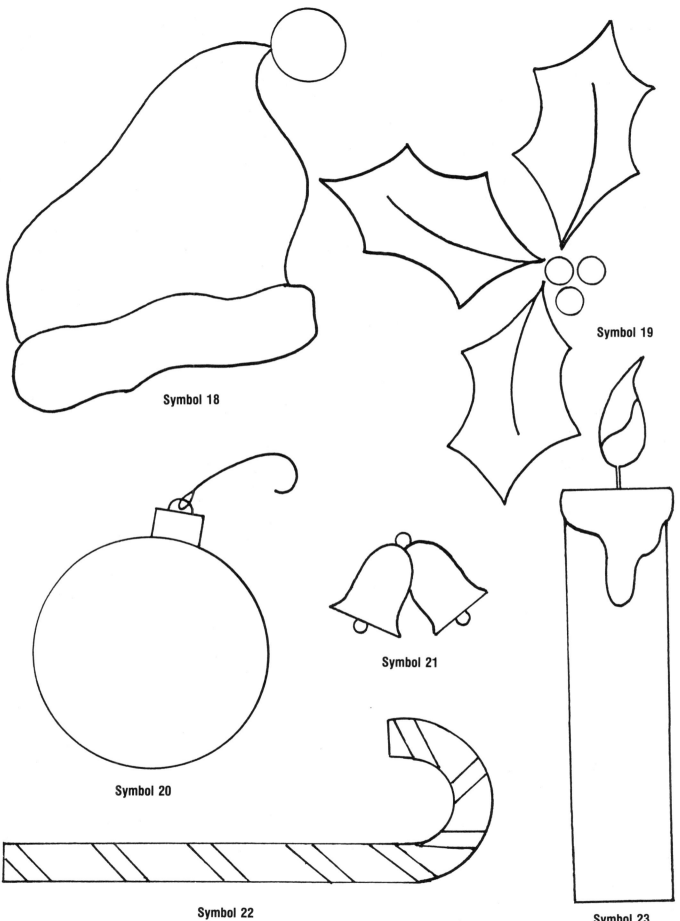

Symbol 18

Symbol 19

Symbol 20

Symbol 21

Symbol 22

Symbol 23

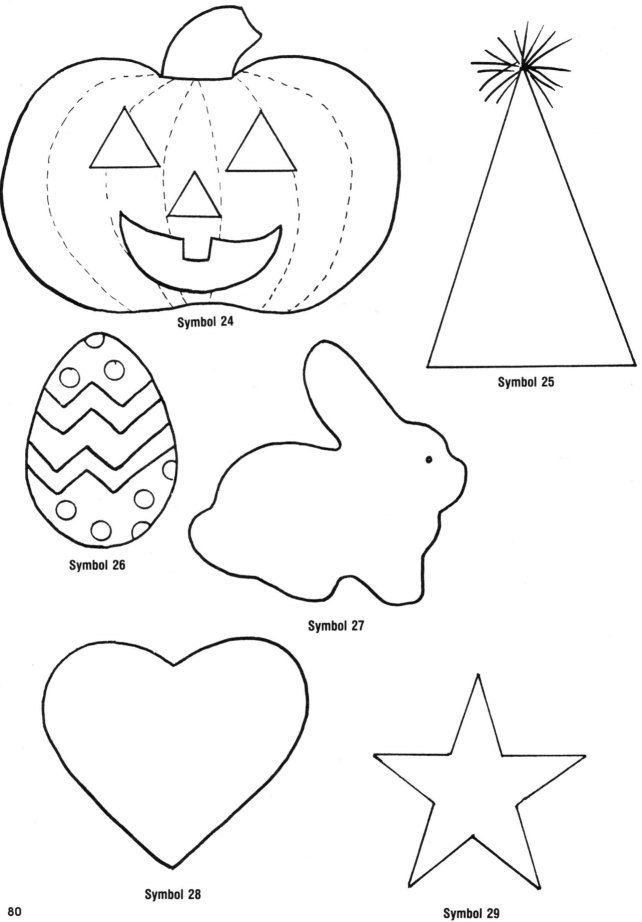

Symbol 24

Symbol 25

Symbol 26

Symbol 27

Symbol 28

Symbol 29